Good Drive.

A No Nonsense Approach to Mastering Google Drive

Table Of Contents

Introduction

I want to thank you and congratulate you for downloading the Good Drive: A No Nonsense Approach to Mastering Google Drive.

This book contains proven steps and strategies on how to use Google Drive to your advantage. You will be amazed at what you can get out of this file storage and synchronization system.

Here's an inescapable fact: you will need to get your data saved properly so you will have access to it well into the future. However, many people often forget about how important it is for them to back it all up on something that is easy to access.

Today you can use Google Drive to store a variety of files on a cloud network. You can share those files with other people and even edit them. You can use this to make yourself more productive.

You will learn throughout this book about a variety of points relating to Google Drive. You'll about not only how to upload items but how to keep tabs on what you can share and how people can access the files you upload. You will also learn about the many applications that you can use to help you edit and adjust your files as needed. This includes a look at how collaboration can work to your advantage when making your setup run properly.

If you do not develop your Google Drive skills then it will certainly be harder for you to keep your business efforts running right. You have to make sure your data is saved properly and that it's all easy to access as needed. You must also make it to where people that you work with and trust can get access to files that you might need a bit of help with.

It's time for you to become an amazing Google Drive expert. Everything that you have wanted to know about using Google Drive is covered in this guide.

Chapter 1 – Getting Ready to Use Google Drive

Choosing to use Google Drive is a smart thing to do in its own right. Let's take a look at how Google Drive can work for your needs.

How It All Works

To enjoy using Google Drive, it helps to get a clear idea of how this system works. Fortunately, the concept of Google Drive is easy to understand.

Google Drive allows you to store your files onto a secure account. This account is hosted by Google, one of the world's top search engines.

As you store your files, you can make them accessible to yourself or other people. You can even adjust the permissions that come with getting these files online.

As you use Google Drive, you can get access to many tools that allow you to edit and share information with people. These include the Google Docs, Sheets and Slides programs that you will learn about a little later in this guide. These programs will let you create and adjust items while sending them out to anyone on your mailing list or those you have given permissions to.

The functions that Google Drive offers let you keep your files secure. They also keep you from losing data. It will also be easier for you to upload items with care when used properly.

Signing Up

You will have to sign up for a Google Drive account before you can start using it. It is very easy to get an account ready for your use. In particular, you can quickly get an account by going to drive.google.com.

You can then log into a proper Google account while you are on the page. You can get your own Google account for free; this will give you access to Gmail and other features.

Of course, this works especially well if you have an Android-powered mobile device. After all, Google has put in a large investment in that mobile operating system.

Getting a Download

Although it is easy for you to get Google Drive to work on a web browser, you should download the main Drive application for use on your desktop. The Drive app is available for PC use and streamlines the overall process of using it. This is especially important as it makes it easier for you to sync files to Drive as desired.

When signing up, you can choose to download an appropriate mobile application so you can get easy access to your Drive account. You can get an Android or iOS version of the app to work for you. You will just have to log into your account through the app to get access to your Drive files from anywhere.

It is free to download the Google Drive app to any device. It will cost money if you use more data, which brings us to the next point.

What Web Browser?

Google Drive will work on just about every web browser out there. However, it is best to use the Google Chrome browser. This is thanks to how it can be adjusted with many add-ons to make Drive even better. You will learn more about these add-ons later in this book.

How Much Data?

You must then think about the total amount of money you'll spend on your Google Drive account. It is free for you to store up to 15 GB on your Google Drive account.

It will cost extra for you to get more data to use on Drive account. It can cost as little as $1.99 per month to get 100 GB of storage. Of course, the cost will increase dramatically if you have even more of a need for storage.

Be sure to think carefully about how much data you need now and in the future. Fortunately, it is easy to switch from one plan to another.

What's On Your Main Page?

As you get onto Google Drive, you will get your own main page to work with. This is where you can access all the files that you have uploaded or saved onto your account.

The page will show you what you have, who owns the document and when it was last modified alongside the file size. You can also sort through your data based on when it was last updated and so forth. You also have the option to put items into your trash and eventually permanently delete them if you no longer have a need for them.

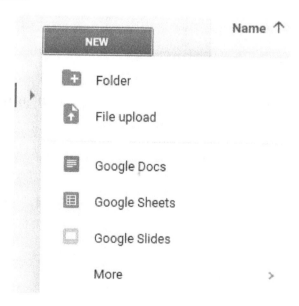

The New button will be important to look at. This will give you the option to upload a file or to even create a new folder.

It is best to create a series of folders to make it easier for you to sort your files out. These can be sorted based on things like what is in the files, who sent them and so forth.

The New button also allows you to get access to different Google Drive programs like Docs and Slides. This allows you to create different files as you see fit.

By using the interface properly, you can get access to all the things that you want to use at a given time. It is very easy to use the Google Drive interface no matter what device you access it on.

What About Photos and Mail?

An important point to see with your Google Drive account is that it includes three different points that can determine the amount of data you are using:

1. Your Drive files

2. Your Gmail account; this is the one you access through the Gmail portal and is linked to the same account that you are using Drive through

3. Your Google Photos; you can easily access these photos through the left-hand side of the Drive screen

You must put all of these points into consideration when getting your Drive account ready. This is to see that you don't use more data than whatever it is you might be able to afford.

Remember when using Google Drive that you have full control over everything you want to do with it. It is a great program and feature that you can use with your Google account right now to keep your data and information under control.

Chapter 2 – Getting Files Online and Syncing Them

It doesn't take much for you to get your files online. The process for getting everything online is very easy to follow.

There are two options you can consider. You can upload files on your own or you can get them to be automatically synced onto your account.

Uploading Files

The manual process for uploading files is perfect for when you have very specific files that need to be saved right now.

1. Click the New button.

2. Choose the File Upload option.

3. Select whatever file it is you want to upload. The dialog box should be similar to what you'd see on most other applications on your computer or mobile device.

4. Check the bottom right part of the screen. This will show the status of your uploads.

5. The file should be on your account after this.

Name ↑	Owner	Last modified	File size
1-16-16	me	Jan 25, 2016 me	—
1-2-16	me	Jan 25, 2016 me	—
mf	me	Aug 27, 2013 me	—
CarowindsParkMap.pdf	me	9:54 AM me	9 MB

My Drive ▾

This is an amazingly easy to use process. It only takes a few moments to do this although it takes longer for files to be uploaded depending on how big they are. Regardless, this is a very effective process that is very simple for anyone to work with.

Syncing Files

Another option to consider is to sync the files that come onto your computer. This works when you have downloaded the Google Drive program onto your computer.

1. You'll have to click on the Google Drive icon on your program.

This is what the icon looks like. If you're using a PC, you can access this on the bottom right part of the screen. On a Mac, it is on the top right part of the screen.

2. You will have to go to the Sync Options menu through the Preferences.

3. You can choose to sync files on your drive or a series of folders. Choose to have either everything on your hard drive synced up to your Drive account or just a few folders.

12

Make sure you choose things carefully. Depending on what happens on the hard drive on your computer, you might have to reconfigure your syncing settings in the event that you move one file folder to another part of your physical drive.

When syncing your data, you can choose to get your content saved in any manner that you see fit. You can choose to get your data synced by limiting the total changes that might take place. You can choose to get your data synced up at certain times in the day. You can also establish limits as to how big the data can be.

Syncing Other Cloud Setups

It is always advisable to have your files set up on several backup accounts. This is to add more protection your files in the event that one backup becomes problematic for whatever reason. Fortunately, Google Drive can sync up to your Dropbox, OneDrive or other added cloud account with ease.

When using Google Drive, you will have to choose to give Drive access to your other cloud files. This can be done by selecting the designated cloud folder that is on your computer.

This will allow you to link the Drive account with whatever that cloud folder might be. This should be simple enough to use in most cases.

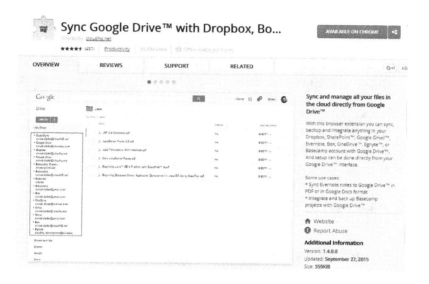

You might also want to download the cloud HQ extension for the Google Chrome web browser. This should be useful for most of your accounts but you will have to pay extra depending on the amount of data that has to be saved. The initial download is still free.

Chapter 3 – Managing Your Files

Getting your files onto a Google Drive account is easy to do. You need to know how you can go about with managing those files though. There are a number of good considerations to use when getting your files managed to be as easy to follow as possible.

Create Folders

As you saw in the last chapter, you can easily create a variety of folders that can be used to store data in. In particular, you can get these folders to work with as many files as needed. You can also choose to move or upload files to certain folders, thus making it easier for you to get your data organized.

The Add button is the key way to go at this point. You can use the button to add individual folders all around the place. Think of this as if it were you adjusting your hard drive with different folders all around.

You will have the option to name your file folders anything you want. This is perfect if you're trying to divide your folders based on the content of files, when they are being added and so forth.

Managing Your Trash

Like with any other computer or mobile device, you will have a trash bin to work with. This will allow you to delete files or folders as needed.

You can right-click on a file to delete it (you would have to keep your finger on a file if you're using a mobile device) and send it to your trash.

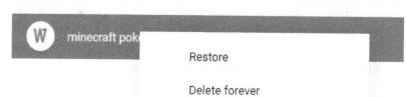

You can then go to the trash menu and choose to do one of two things:

1. You can choose to restore the file by putting it back into the folder or other section on your Drive.

2. You can also get your file deleted forever. This saves space but it will eliminate your file altogether.

Be responsible with your trash. The contents of your trash will still count as part of the storage space that you are using.

Search For Files

While it is true that you can use the many folders on your account to get access to all the stuff you've got, you might want to be careful. It can be easy to lose track of your files. Of course, there is always the case that you might have uploaded something in the past but you don't really remember anywhere about where you put it.

You can use a search feature on Google Drive to find the file. This can be found through the top part of the program. This works in that you just have to enter in the file name or keyword relating to that file. This will help you look to see what's in Drive account.

Be advised that Google Drive does not necessarily look through every single keyword or point within a file. It focuses on the author of a file, the name of that file and so forth. Try and be as specific as possible when searching for a file so you will at least have an easier shot with finding the file that you want.

You can also use the Info icon to give yourself details on whatever you have done in recent time. This can work if you're trying to find something you opened.

This Info icon can be found on the top right part of your screen. This will list information on all the things you have done with your account at a given time.

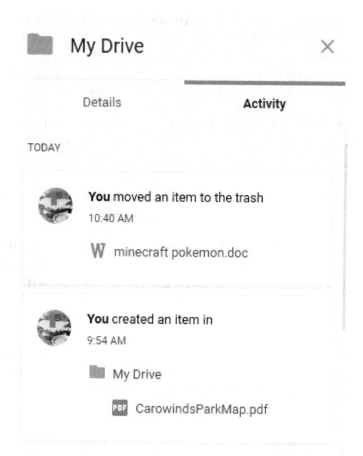

You can use this to help you recall what you might have done in the past. This can help you to keep whatever you have sorted out properly so it won't be too hard for you to get your data organized in some way.

Managing Older Versions

One convenient part of Google Drive is that it will take in any edits that might have been made through the Google Docs program or other attached programs.

This allows you to compare different versions and see how different they might be from one another.

An especially popular feature of this is that the Google Drive program will keep tabs on edits or changes to a file, when a file is renamed, when files are moved and so forth.

This can make it easier for you to get your data managed the right way while also keeping tabs on what's going on with a file.

You will have to use the Info icon to see what changes have been made. You can right-click or hold down the file to get access to different file versions.

Google Drive can hold onto older versions of a file for up to thirty days after they are created. This should give you enough time to take a closer look at the assorted changes that might have been made to your files.

As you use this, it should be rather easy for you to get your files to be easier to read. Make sure you use this part of the program carefully so it will not be too hard for you to get access to the many files and other features that you want to work with.

Chapter 4 – Using Apps With Drive

You can use a variety of great applications with your Google Drive account. These applications will help you to get the most out of the files you're using.

There are many great applications that can work right now. Some of them are offered by Google. Others are from different companies but it's easy to use them with Drive.

What Google Offers

Google offers a variety of different tools that can be used to help you create and share content with each other. While it is true that you can use Microsoft Office and OpenOffice files on Drive, you should certainly consider Google's productivity tools instead.

The reason for this is because Google Drive offers apps that allow you to quickly edit a program through the Drive account that you access. The older versions of whatever you have on a Drive account can be accessed as well.

Here's a look at the many programs that Google has to offer:

- Docs lets you create traditional documents. You can create and edit word files.

- Sheets is a spreadsheet program. You can use this to create different files that allow you to keep technical data organized properly

- Slides is a presentation program similar to PowerPoint. You can create presentations that can be used to convey information through slides.

- Forms lets you create surveys and analyze how they are being used. You can use this to keep tabs on how people are answering the questions in surveys as well.

- Drawings allows you to create your own drawings, diagrams or other visual display features. This is perfect for when you're trying to create visual designs of certain things.

All of these programs are free to use. You can save the information that you generate onto your Drive account.

Best of all, you don't have to download any new software if you don't feel like it. You can access these programs right off of your Drive account by clicking on the New section and choosing the proper program that you want to open. You can also save the files that you create on your own.

This is a very convenient and useful feature but it helps to get a good hang of the programs before you really start to commit to them. Fortunately, these programs work in just about the same way as many of the other programs that you might normally use with productive needs in mind. This is a great point to see when you are aiming to get the most out of your apps.

Working With Office Files

You can easily get Microsoft Office files loaded onto your Drive setup. This is great if you prefer to use Office instead of one of the apps that Google has provided to you.

You need to install a proper Google Drive plug-in for Office to make it work. You can visit https://tools.google.com/dlpage/driveforoffice to get your Google Drive plug-in installed.

This will allow you to save your files to your hard drive or directly to your Google Drive. Therefore, you can keep your physical hard drive from being filled with too much space as your Google Drive will take everything.

This works for Word, Excel, PowerPoint and Outlook.

Also, to open a file from Drive through an Office program, you will have to go to the Open from Google Drive section to get access to your Drive files. The prompt should be right next to the one that lets you access normal files.

You can also choose to open up the Office file directly from the Drive account and then choose to open it with Docs. A bar on the top of the screen will give you several options for how you are going to access a file.

Notice on the bar that you can choose the Open option to load up the file in Docs. You can always print it out, send it to other people or download it right to your hard drive if you prefer. Either way, whatever you have to offer will be fully visible and easy for you to generate.

Using Yahoo Mail

It is clear that you can get your Drive files to go into your Gmail messages with ease. The Drive icon on your email can allow you to get access to your Drive files so you can choose whatever it is you want to send out to someone in real time. however, Gmail is not the only email option that you can use as well.

You can get your Google Drive account to sync with your Yahoo Mail account. This works for those who have the Yahoo Mail and Google Drive applications on their mobile devices.

You can link your Drive to your Yahoo Mail profile by using the following steps:

1. Open your Yahoo Mail app.

2. As you write your new mail, go to the attachment icon.

3. Tap on the Cloud Storage option.

4. Add the Google Drive account to your Yahoo Mail by logging into Drive through Ymail.

5. Make sure you choose to allow access.

This ensures that you can get Ymail to link to your Drive. You can also go to a section on your device that lets you manage your apps and choose to disconnect the Drive from Ymail at a later time.

After you get Ymail linked up, you can take any file you have through your Drive and have it work on this popular mobile mail platform.

Linking to Evernote

Evernote is a popular website that lets you draft notes and use them in presentations for business or personal needs. You can get your Drive files to link up to your Evernote account right now.

To use Google Drive with Evernote, you must click on the proper Drive icon on any note that you have created and want to attach a file onto. Evernote offers full support for Drive so it should be easy for you to make this work.

You will be asked to log onto your Drive account if you have not attached anything onto an Evernote posting before. Fortunately, this is very easy to do as it only takes a few moments for you to get this to work.

Don't Forget Add-Ons

A great thing about Google Drive is that you can add a variety of additional programs to help you make it run even better. These add-ons are unique in that they will let you add extensions to your Chrome browser. These can automatically be installed onto your browser and can also be uninstalled through the preferences menu on your browser.

These add-ons typically work as options that make it easier for you to adjust files through your Drive account. These in turn should help you to get the most out of whatever you are creating.

Be advised that you will need Chrome browser to get many of these add-ons to work, what with Google being the group directly behind the browser.

Also, you should encourage people who get access to your files to also use these add-ons. This is just to get everyone on the same page.

Here are a few of these add-ons that can especially help. A majority of these are free to use but some will cost you money depending on how you use them or what plans you might enter into:

- Google Translate allows you to translate different items into a foreign language. You can even translate foreign documents to your own language.

- The Calculator add-on lets you access a camera through the Drive setup. This is perfect for when you are working on a file in Sheets and you need help with entering or calculating data. Best of all, you don't have to fiddle between windows to use this app.

- The AbleBits Suite helps you with five different programs to assist you in making spreadsheets easier to manage. You can separate values into different cells or merge them together, for instance. You can also find fuzzy matches where certain variations on specific terms might be found.

- HelloFax lets you fax a document right off of Google Docs. This is convenient but it costs one dollar per fax or ten dollars for an unlimited total every month.

- HelloSign lets you add signature prompts onto your Drive files. You can get this added onto up to three documents each month for free. It costs $15 per month to get an unlimited number of documents to work with this feature.

Other options are always being made available. Be sure to look around to see what you can use when finding ways to get the most out of your Drive programs.

The functionality that comes with Google Drive is great for you to check out. Make sure you look at how you can use Google Drive so you can get more out of whatever you are trying to load up.

Chapter 5 – Collaboration and Adjusting Permissions

One of the most popular parts of Google Drive comes from how you can use this to allow a variety of people to get access to your files. That is, you can give other people permission to view what's on your Drive account.

Google Drive allows you to collaborate with other people on different files. You can get up to fifty people to access a document at the same time. In addition, up to 200 people can share a file.

Even with this, you must see that the permissions being used when accessing Google Drive files are managed properly. This is to keep only those who actually have access to your Google Drive files to use what you have.

Getting People To Access Files

To start the collaboration process, you need to give people access to the files that you want to work with. The process for doing this is rather easy to follow.

27

1. Make sure you log into your Drive account.

2. Choose the proper file that you want people to access.

3. Right-click or hold onto the file and then choose the Share option.

4. You can then enter in the email addresses of all those that you want to give your file out to. You can manually enter in addresses or you can add the names of those who are already in your Google Mail address book.

As the file is being shared, all people who have access to it will be able to look at the same file. That is, there is just one file to work with as the risk of several people using the same file and saving their own pieces of information and creating too many versions of it will be reduced. You will have a much easier time with using your data and getting the program to work for you when this is all considered.

Editing In Real Time

Google Drive can be used by many people at the same time to access individual files and work on them. This means that people can be at different computers and still see how files might be changed in real time. This allows people to quickly see what is going on when trying to change data or information on a file.

This is great to see but you should look at the formatting that works beforehand. You can allow people to edit Docs, Sheets and other Google-related files. For Office files, people will have to either open them directly through their Office programs or they can get them converted to be read on Docs or other apps.

Actually, the file format should not change no matter what option you choose. The interface and the ability of a file to be read may be temporarily changed but you will not have to worry about whether or not a file can be read by other programs based on how you are changing things around in them.

Permissions

Permissions are important to think about with regards to how you're going to get Google Drive to work for you. You can always adjust the permissions that someone has for an account by using one of three options.

1. A person can edit the file.

2. That person can comment on the file. That is, the person can leave comments on what to do with a file but will not be able to actually carry out the suggestions.

3. The person can simply view the file.

These three options go from having the most control to the least. While a user will still get access to an account, it is important to see how well the control setup is going when making it all work right.

You can adjust the permissions by choosing that person's ability to access a file while entering in the email address. You can choose from each of these three options in the drop down menu.

After adding individual names, you can choose to adjust the permissions on the fly. You can select the blue label on the right-hand side of each person's name to adjust the permission that comes with the file.

The best part about this is that you can use individual settings for every file and folder that you have to work with. Therefore, you can choose to let people get access to very specific parts of your account if necessary. This is perfect if there are certain files that you want to keep off-limits from those who might already be accessing other files.

An Important Collaborative Tip

No matter how the collaboration process works, you have to see that it's being organized and that everyone is held accountable. Google Drive lets you do just that.

Google Drive will share edit information on all the files you have for people to read. The information will stay online for 30 days after it is created. This allows you to have plenty of time to adjust information and change things around on the fly as you might see fit.

Be sure to check the individual edits that might have come about as you file has been made available. This can help you see who is doing things right and who needs a little bit of help. This is also to see that you can take in older versions of a file in the event that several people do something the wrong way.

Using Chat

One of the best things you can do when using the collaborative features on Google Drive is to chat with people.

The chat box on Google Drive can open while you are busy using a proper Google-based program like Docs. You can use the dialog box on the top right part of a program to open up a listing that shows you and the names of those who have access to the file. This will then show you who is online to see if it necessary.

akern

mikechang

me: Should we expand this survey to director level?

mikechang: Yes lets add another section, I'm adding a few questions, jump in on the multiple choice response options

Type here to chat

You can then chat with that person if there is someone who is online who is using the same file. You can simply load up the file and talk with that person in real time.

This is perfect as it makes it easier for you to get in touch with someone about the edits that have to be done in real time. Best of all, you don't have to get a webcam or microphone ready to take care of the work. You won't have to worry about spending lots of time on the phone either.

Colors For Collaboration

One good idea for your collaborative needs is to think about the colors that people can be linked up to. That is, the edits that people can make may be distinguished by a series of colored bars or marks on a document.

This allows you to clearly look and see just who was responsible for certain edits. You can use this to especially contact those people directly to let them know if the edits or changes they are working with are sensible or not.

What About Larger Groups?

While being able to share your documents with up to 200 people can be great, there is always a good chance that you might want to share your data with an even bigger group of people. With this in mind, you can use a link-sharing feature.

This part of collaboration allows you to share your files with larger groups of people. You can use this for as many people as you want.

This works especially well if you have a very large file that cannot be easily sent by email. This is the case for video or audio files.

You can use these steps to get a link ready:

1. Click on the proper file that you want to share.

2. Go to the link-shaped icon at the top of the screen or page.

3. Click on the icon. This will generate a unique URL that will link up directly to your file.

4. You can then send the link out to anyone. You can send it to people in your address book, other people who ask for it or even on a public website.

The key about this is to let you share things that might otherwise be a challenge to share. This works if you have big documents that cannot be easily sent out through some more traditional means of reaching people.

Collaboration can certainly be great but you have to be certain when doing this right that you know what you are going to get out it. Make sure you use the right setup for letting people access your files and that only the right people can do so thanks to the permissions that you might add.

Chapter 6 – Additional Tips

You have read about all sorts of great things that you can do with Google Drive throughout this guide. Well, there are plenty of other great things that deserve to be seen with regards to how you can make Google Drive work wonders for you.

Use Drag and Drop

It might be easier for you to upload files if you use a drag and drop option. You can drag icons that show your files and drop them onto the Google Drive list. This works well when you have Drive on in the back while a menu with your files on it is on top.

These files will automatically be uploaded to your account when done properly. Be sure to organize these files after you drop them so they are in their right folders.

One related tip is to click and hold onto a file and then drag it to individual folders if you prefer. This lets you quickly move files into the right folders based on what you prefer.

Get Access Offline

There might be times when you need to get access to your files but you cannot do so because you are offline. You can always download the Google Drive Web app for Chrome use. This works well for Chrome browser users in that you can read your files even when you don't have an online connection.

This means that you can edit and adjust your files while on the go. You are no longer bound to just having a single online connection to actually make what you have work.

Use Gmail To Search

You can also use Gmail to search for files in your Google Drive account. This is perfect for when you need to get an email sent out while finding the file you want to use right now.

As you get the search results on your Gmail page, you can click on the proper file. This will lead you to a URL that you can share with someone. This allows a person to look at the file after you send it. You can always adjust the permission that comes with it too.

Convert PDFs Into Text Files

The PDF system is very convenient in that this file format can be read by any computer in the world. However, you need to think about how a PDF can be converted into a text file.

You can use Drive to convert PDFs into text files. You can go to the Upload Settings menu and then choose to upload a PDF and convert the file into a text file. This will work based on the type of file that you are working with.

This can be useful but you have to be careful when getting it to work. You must make sure that the PDF you are working with is fully organized and clear. It has to be easy to read so it will not be hard for you to get an upload ready for your use as needed.

Scan and Upload Photos

Does your mobile device have a scanner or camera? It probably does, what with cameras having become so easy to prepare. Today you can get the photos that you take or scan and upload them to your Drive profile. This can work by using the camera app on your device and using it to link up to your Drive profile.

You can use the option to move your photos to a Drive account if you have it set up for use. Make sure your device is logged into your Drive account so you can easily get this to work for you.

Use Analytics For Surveys

The ability to generate surveys off of the Forms program is very useful. However, you need to see that the data you are generating is suitable and useful. You have to use an appropriate analytics system to make it easier for you to make this run.

You can use the analytics within your Forms account to get a clear idea of who might be taking your survey. This can help you see what the behaviors of other people might be like. Anything that makes it easier for you to figure out what steps you can take after a survey is fully finished can always work.

You should certainly use these tips if you want to get the most out of Google Drive. Make sure these are run properly to give yourself a better total setup that isn't too complicated or hard to use.

Conclusion

Thank you again for downloading this book!

I hope this book was able to help you to see what you can do with the Google Drive system. I feel that this system will work wonders for you when it comes to getting your data saved and made easier for you to access.

Google Drive will indeed make it easier for you to get your data out there and to be easier to use. You can get this to work wonders for when you are trying to get a proper setup ready in terms of getting files to be shared and making them accessible.

The next step is to get to your Google account or create one if you don't have it yet. You can then go to the proper Drive page and then get your files saved up right there. Make sure you look at how you're going to get your files synced up as needed too. This is to help you keep your items under control for as long as possible.

Finally, if you enjoyed this book, please take the time to share your thoughts and post a review on Amazon. It'd be greatly appreciated!

Thank you and good luck!

Summary

Are you looking to keep your files secure? Are you trying to be more productive while letting more people get access to important business-related files?

No matter what you want to do, you can use Google Drive to help you get your files out there in a smart and suitable manner. Google Drive lets you save your documents online and even lets you edit them and create new ones to share with others. You can also collaborate on your documents with other people.

This guide is all about helping you to see how well you can get your files protected through the use of Google Drive and how you can share them. You will learn in this guide about how to get Google Drive to work and how it can be adjusted to your needs. The functions that come with using Google Drive are certainly vast and can be advantageous for when you are trying to get different things to work for you.

Be sure to check out this guide if you want to get the most out of your files. You can use Google Drive anywhere and can edit so many things with it. In fact, you might be surprised at what you can do with it after you read this book. It's a vast service from Google that could be your ally in staying productive while keeping your files protected.

www.ingramcontent.com/pod-product-compliance
Lightning Source LLC
Chambersburg PA
CBHW060934050326
40689CB00013B/3084